PULLING WEEDS
from a
CACTUS GARDEN

Created by
Nathalie Tierce

PULLING WEEDS
from a
CACTUS GARDEN

Created by
Nathalie Tierce

Introduction

I used to worry about the Cold War as an eleven-year-old. The time we watched *The Day After* on TV, about what life would look like after a nuclear bomb, I couldn't get the idea out of my head. There was nothing to help me look at this horror (as real as it was at the time) in perspective.

In the two years I was working on the imagery for *Pulling Weeds From A Cactus Garden,* the world witnessed the most bizarre spectacle of politics. Being in lock-down for Covid-19 made people examine disturbing, deeper currents running through our society in the U.S. that we were otherwise too distracted to scrutinize.

The symbolism that developed in these works came from the turbulence, fear, and confusion we were experiencing and trying to wade our way through.

Lost in a Supermarket

In the eternal daylight,

the aisles lead her trolley

to promises.

She hangs on,

hoping each stop brings her closer to the cure

to make things better.

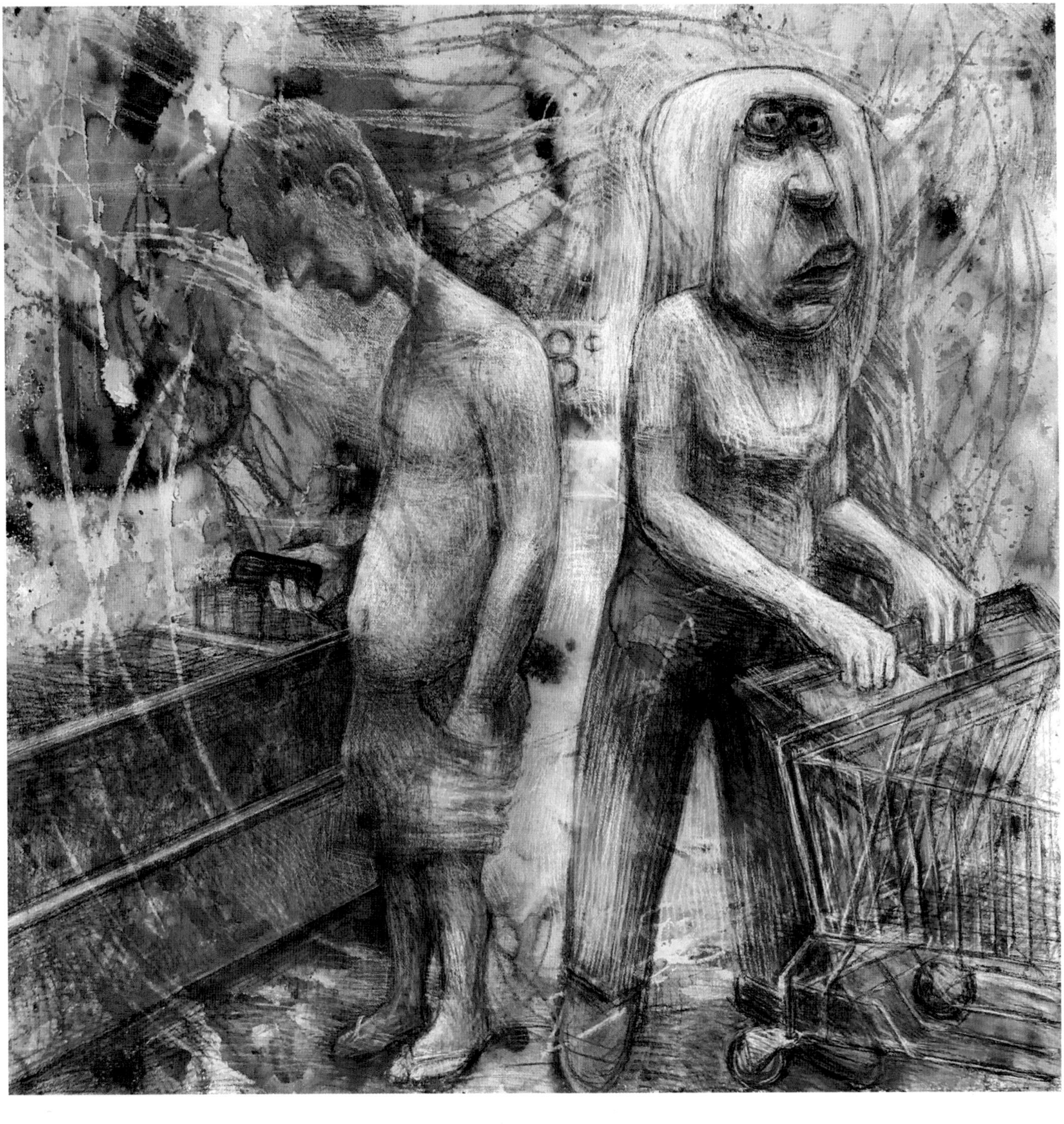
8¢

Domestic Bliss

Pleading, arguing, telling…

Everyone wants to get a word in.

The walls take it and hold it

like an old suitcase

too stuffed with dirty laundry

to close shut.

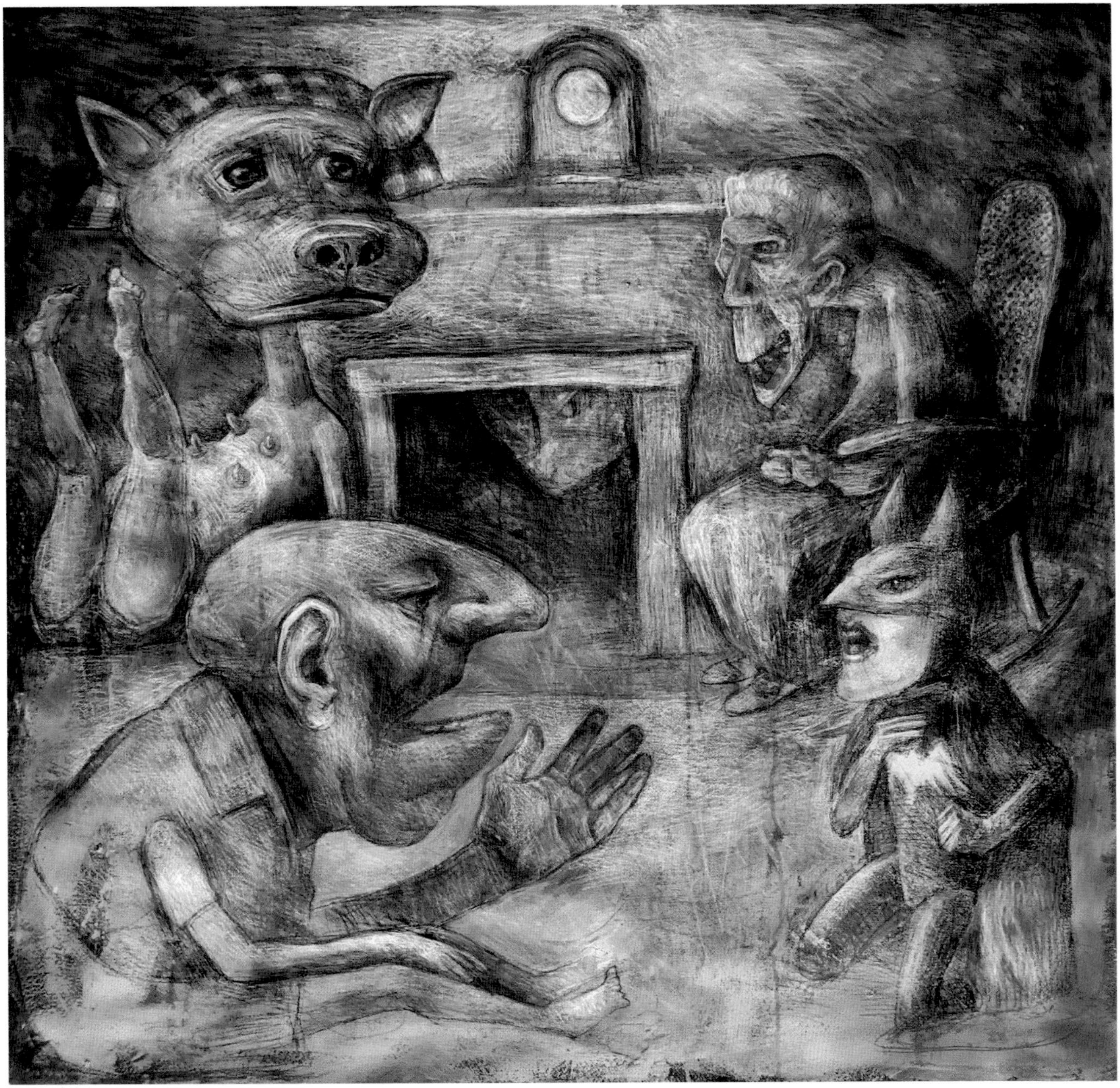

The Young Joker

Noise, speed, excitement…

Chasing shiny things.

How will it end?

There's not much she can do;

the smell of regret is coming…

his final steps are too much to watch.

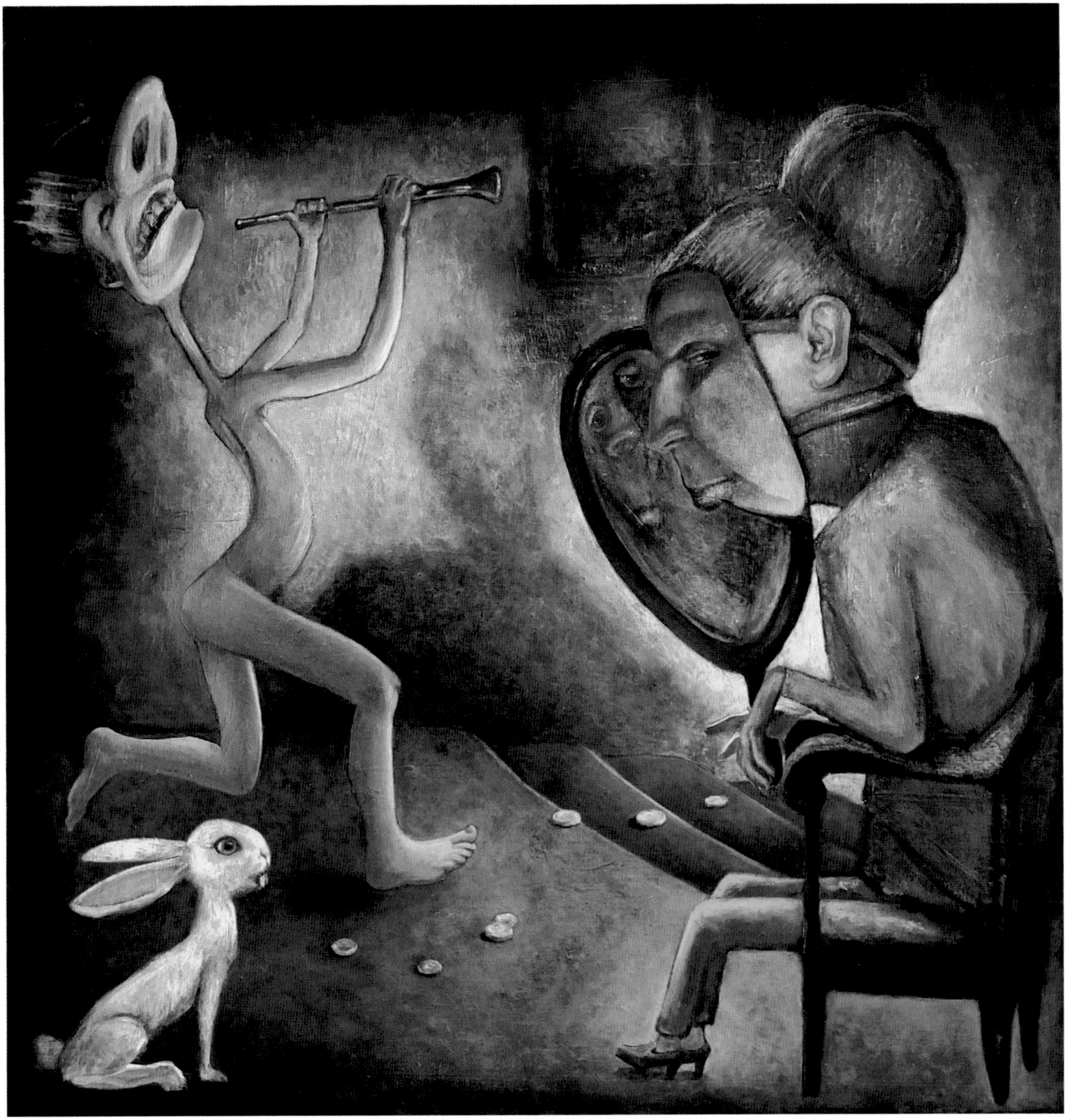

Thoughts on the Outside

Walking around turned inside out,

feeling the coolness of water that's not there.

Just beyond the hospital floor—

that face… I've seen it before…

In the water's reflection? In a glass? A mirror?

I'm not sure anymore.

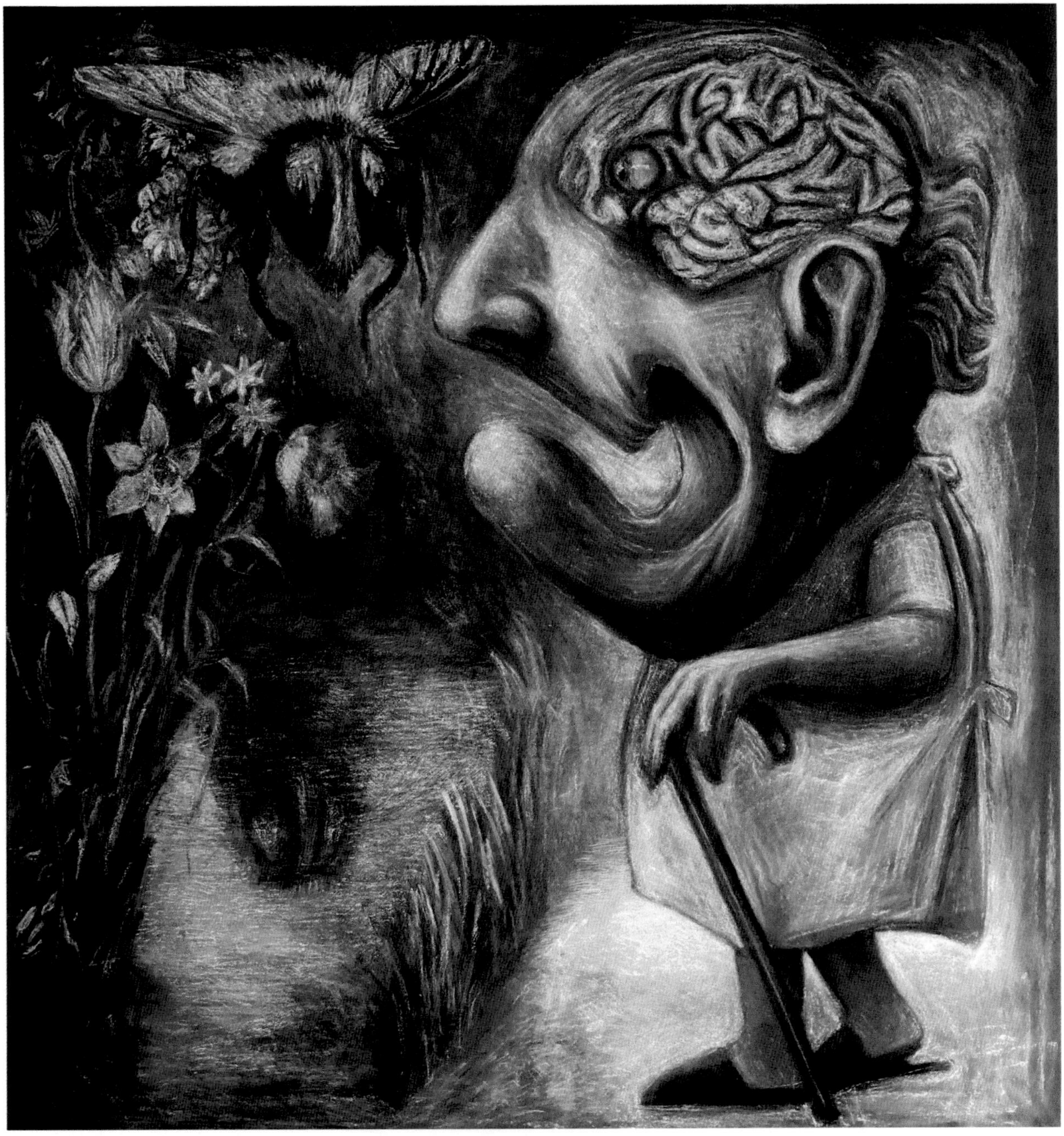

Destiny Guides Our Fortunes

Giants everywhere!

Huge, monstrous warriors.

Worthy opponents we will surely defeat,

gaining great fortune…

You mean those windmills?

Hmpf.

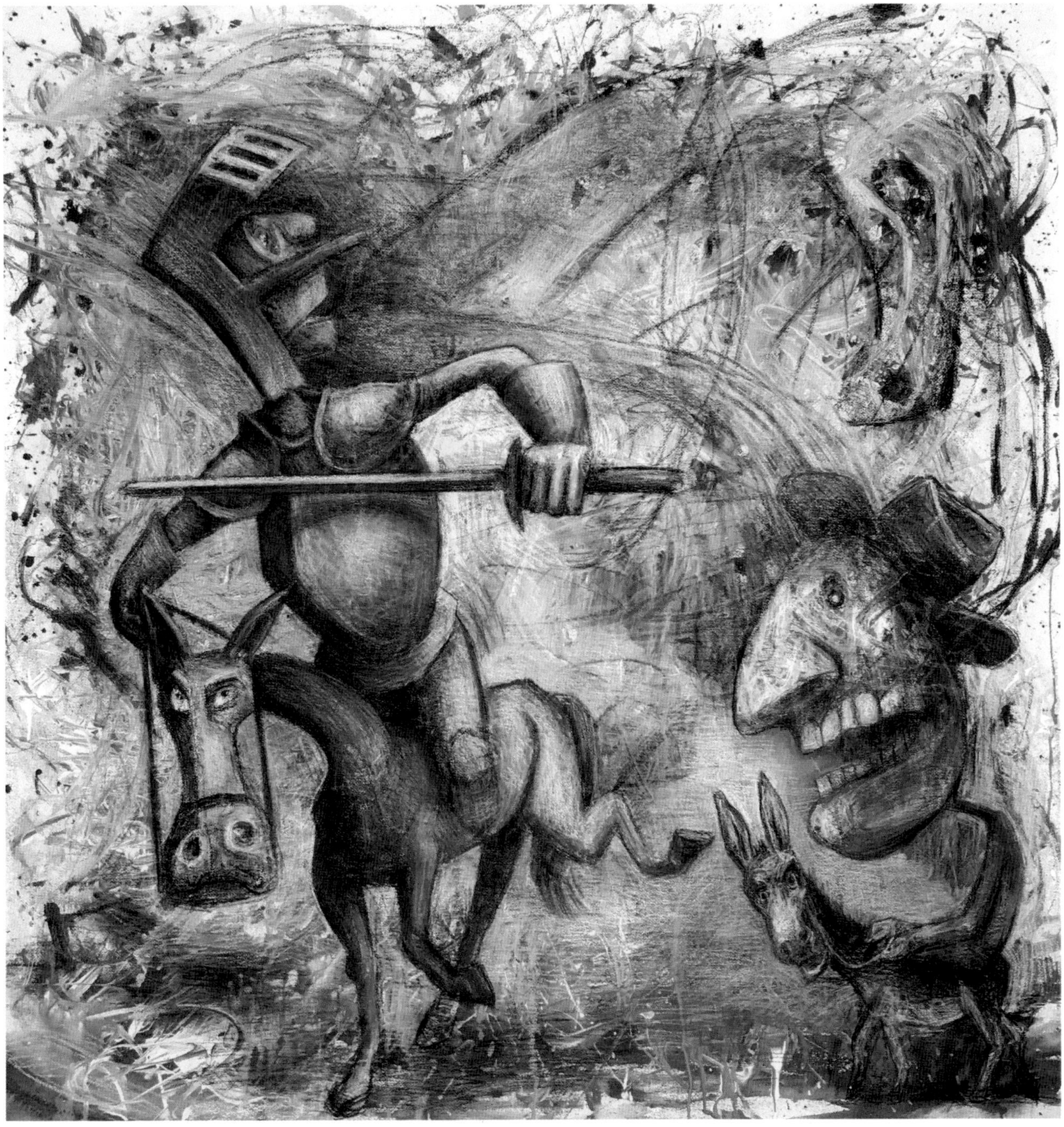

The Show

Waiting for things worth watching…

minutes swell heavy in the stale air.

Send us with a thrill to another place—

Not here. Not us.

Hope wells up in our guts,

lit by stage vapors

mixed with spotlights of despair.

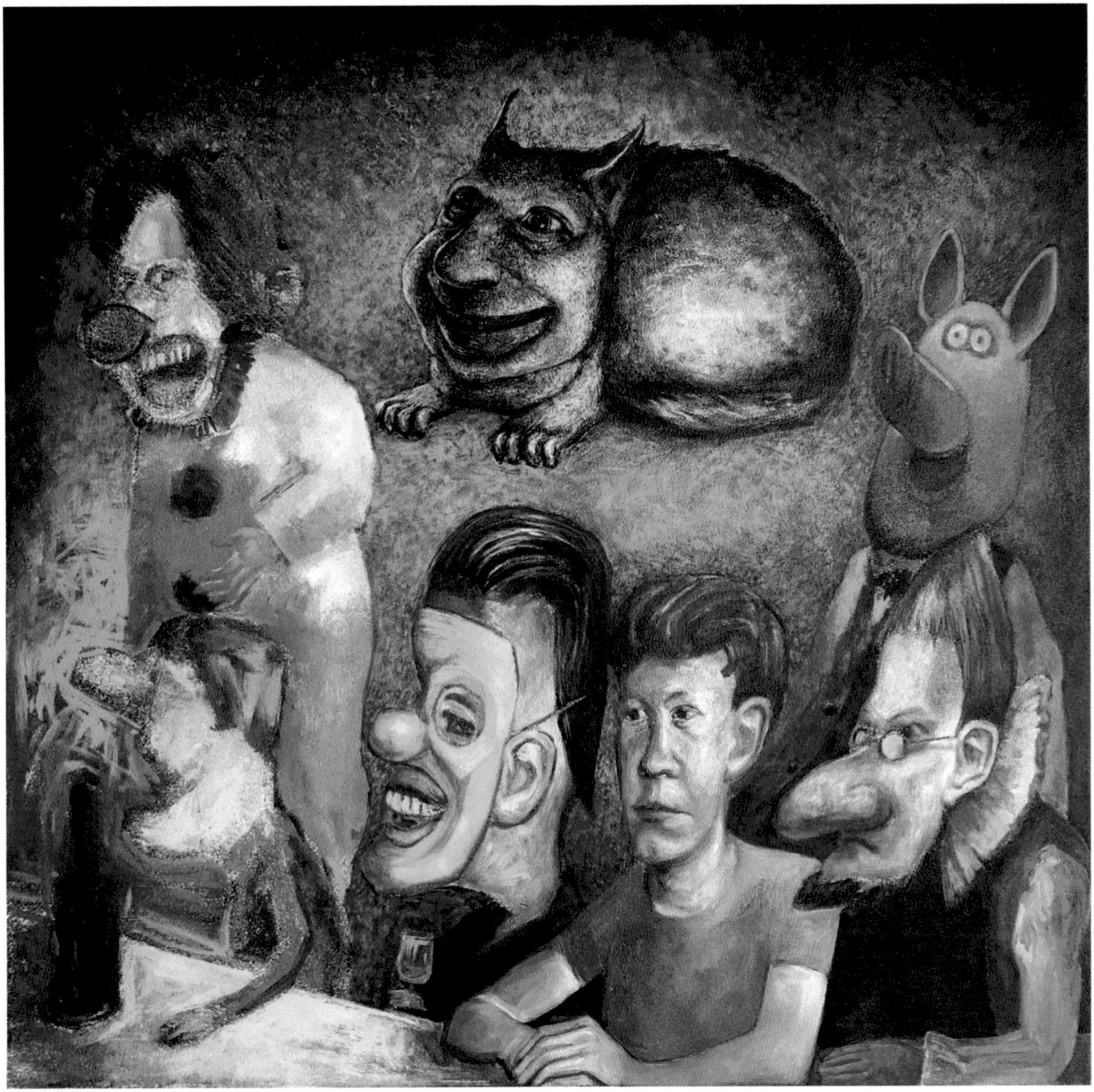

Say No Meore

Ready to snuff your candle glow,

your next word will be your funeral.

Eyes meet, hearing nothing.

Locked in for battle,

panic rules.

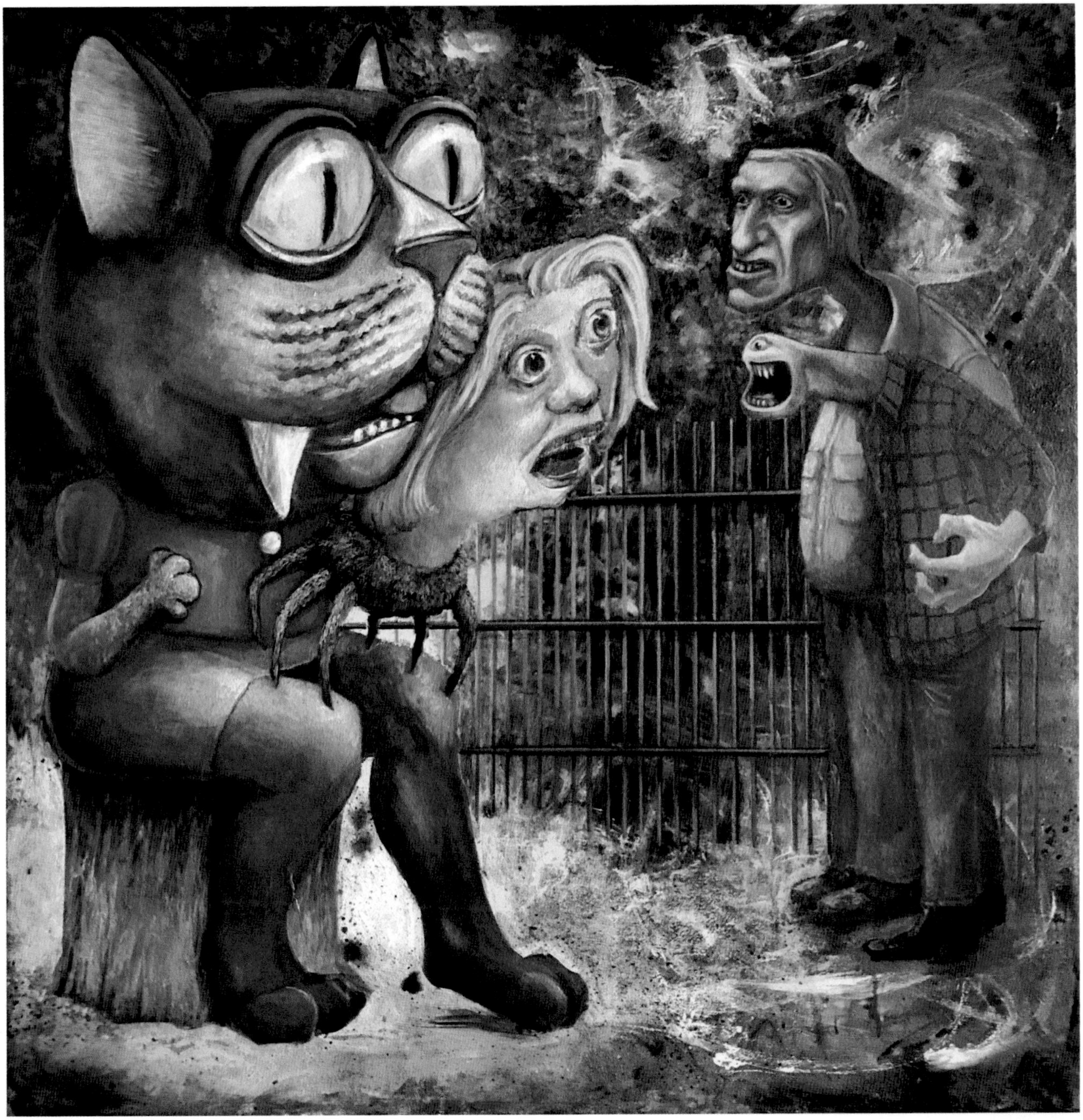

Standoff on the Island

Grab, take, steal…

See nothing.

This is mine.

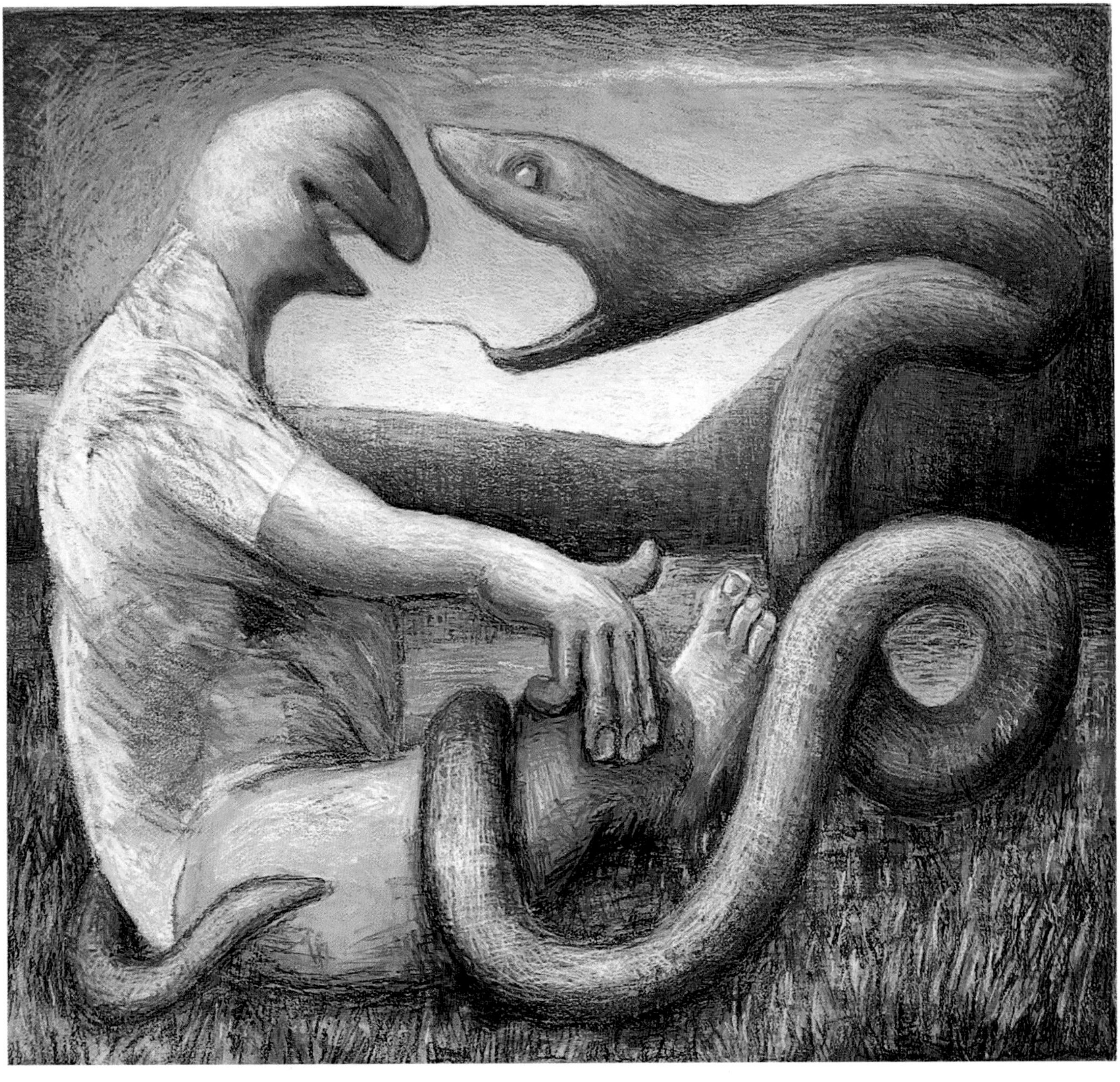

The Lamb and the Wolf

(From Aesop's Fables)

No, that's not my cousin;

I don't know what you're talking about.

It wasn't me either; it's not me that you want…

There's been a mistake.

The drool on your chin

tells me you're not listening.

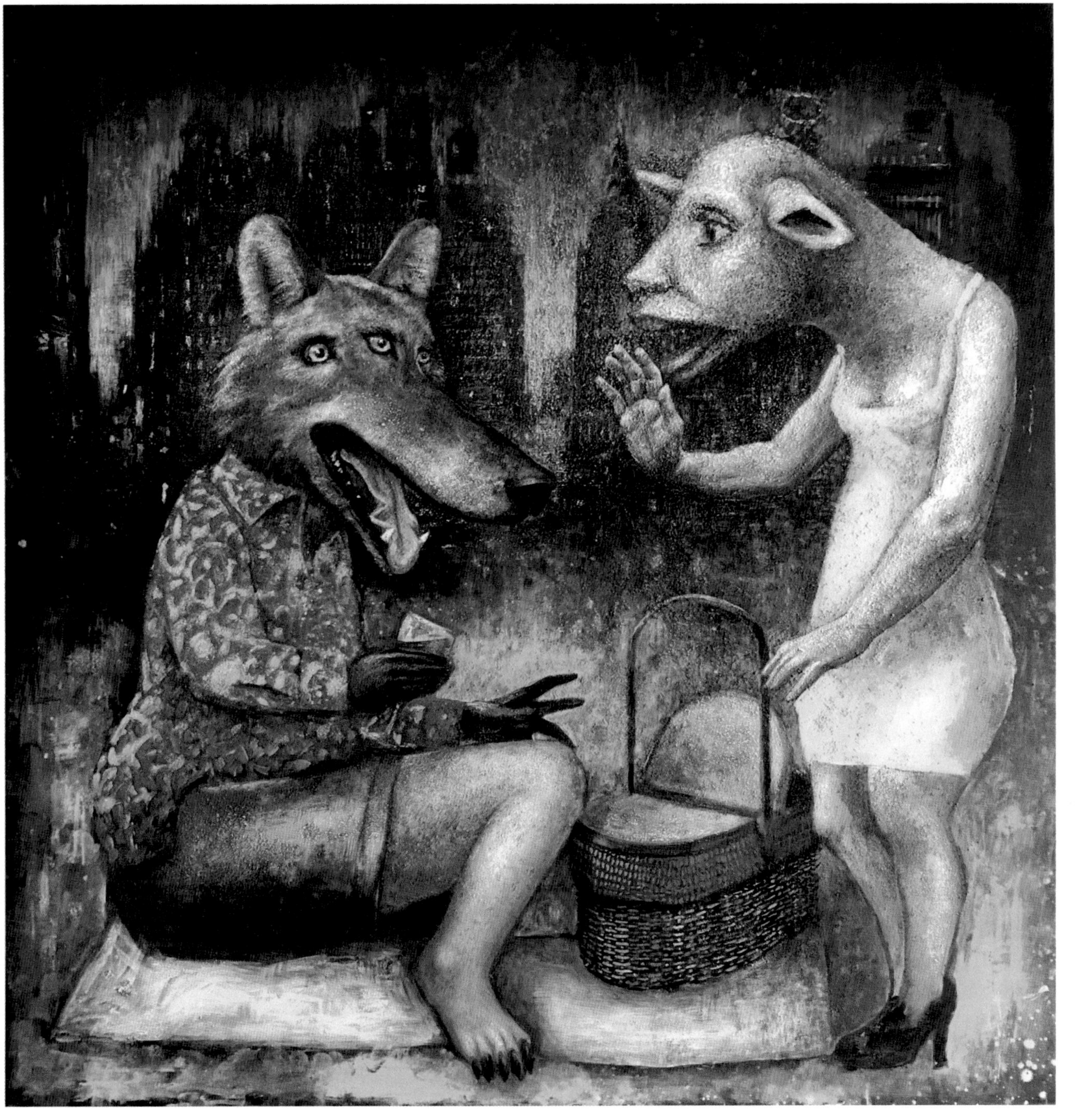

Fireside Dance

Weaving and bobbing,

night air fans the flames.

Yellow sparks crackle—

magic sewn from frenzied steps

sealed by heat.

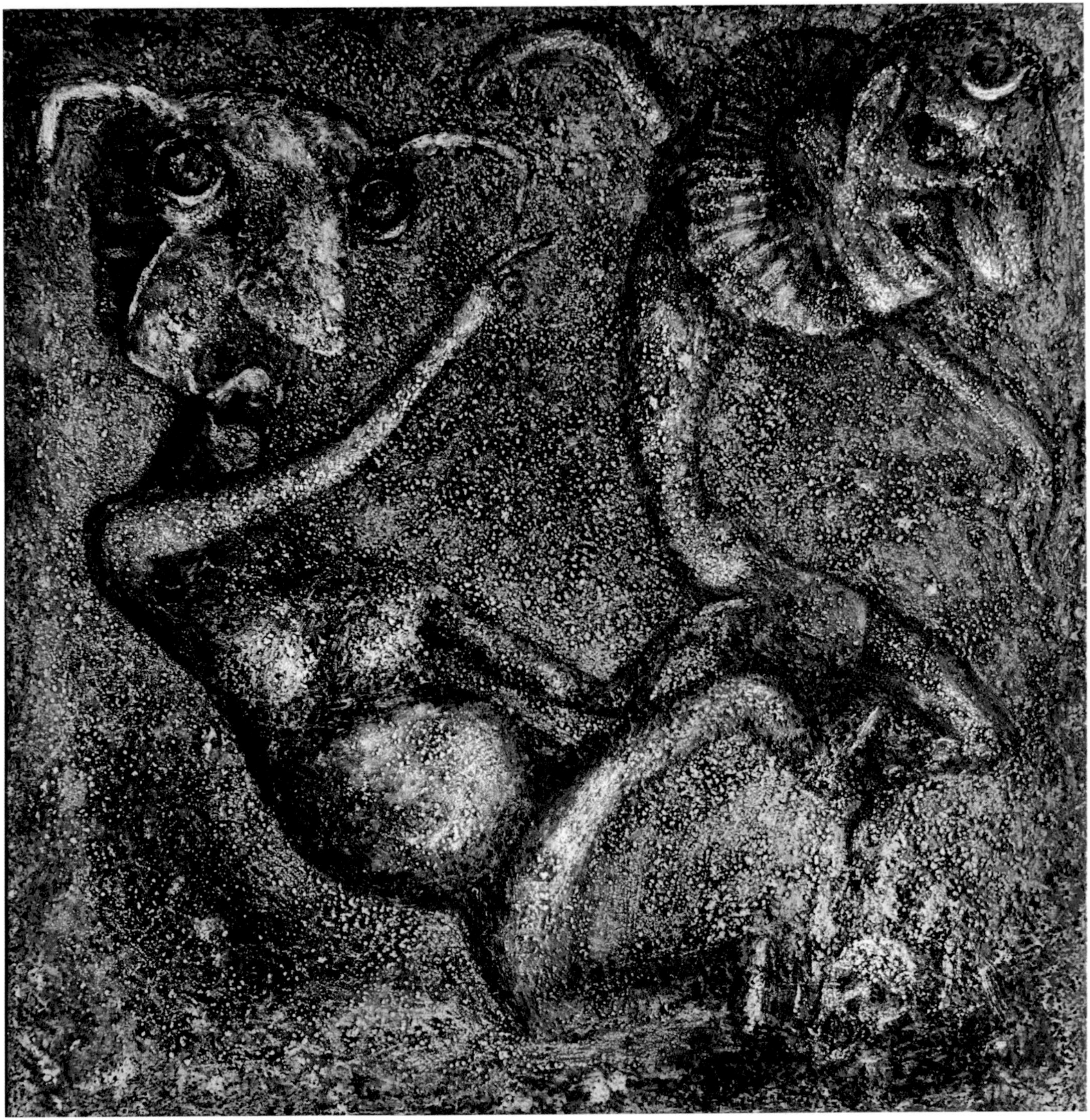

The Fox and the Mosquitoes
(From Aesop's Fables)

That kiss packs a punch!

Hit me harder than anything else I ever felt.

Is this love or anaphylactic shock?

Don't shoo her away…

I don't want another to take her place.

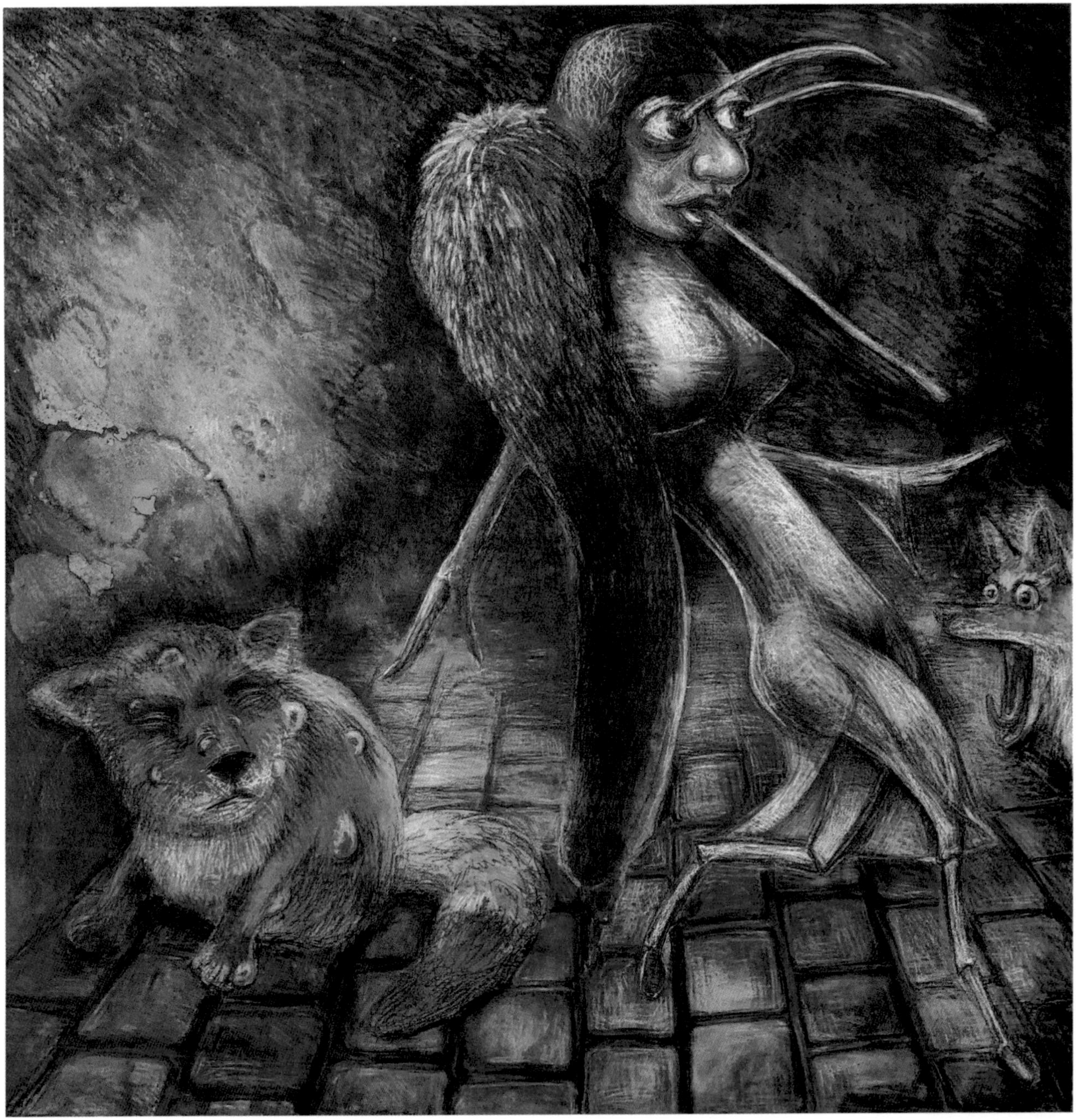

Wolf in Lamb's Clothing

(From Aesop's Fables)

It's almost too easy…

That's part of the thrill.

Just another one of the crowd.

But I'm not;

the crowd is me.

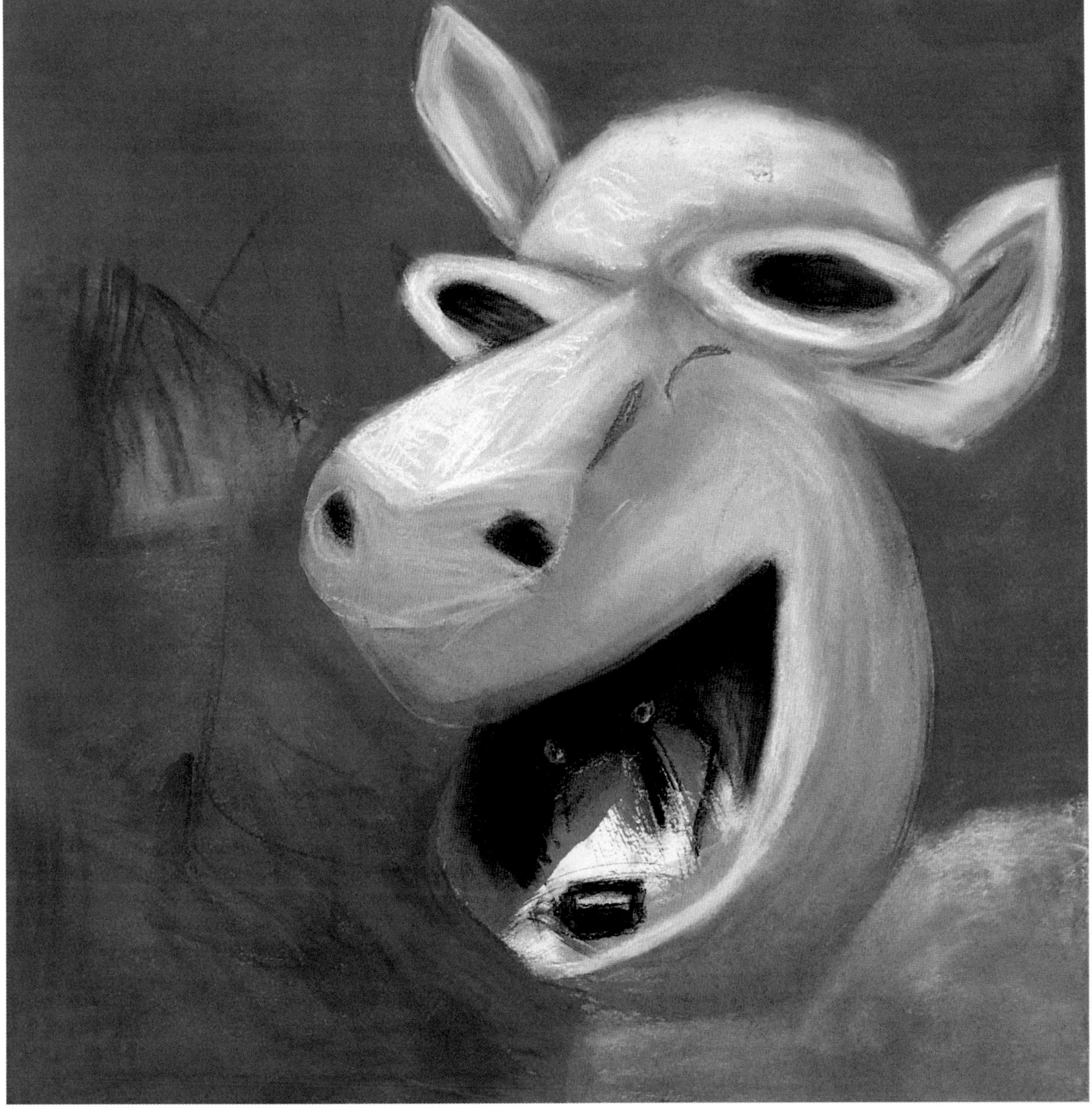

Swamp Thing

Where the hell did you come from?

A sideways glance… an inhaled shriek.

Seconds slip while the mind reels…

What foul wind blew you this way?

Drag your slimy tail somewhere else.

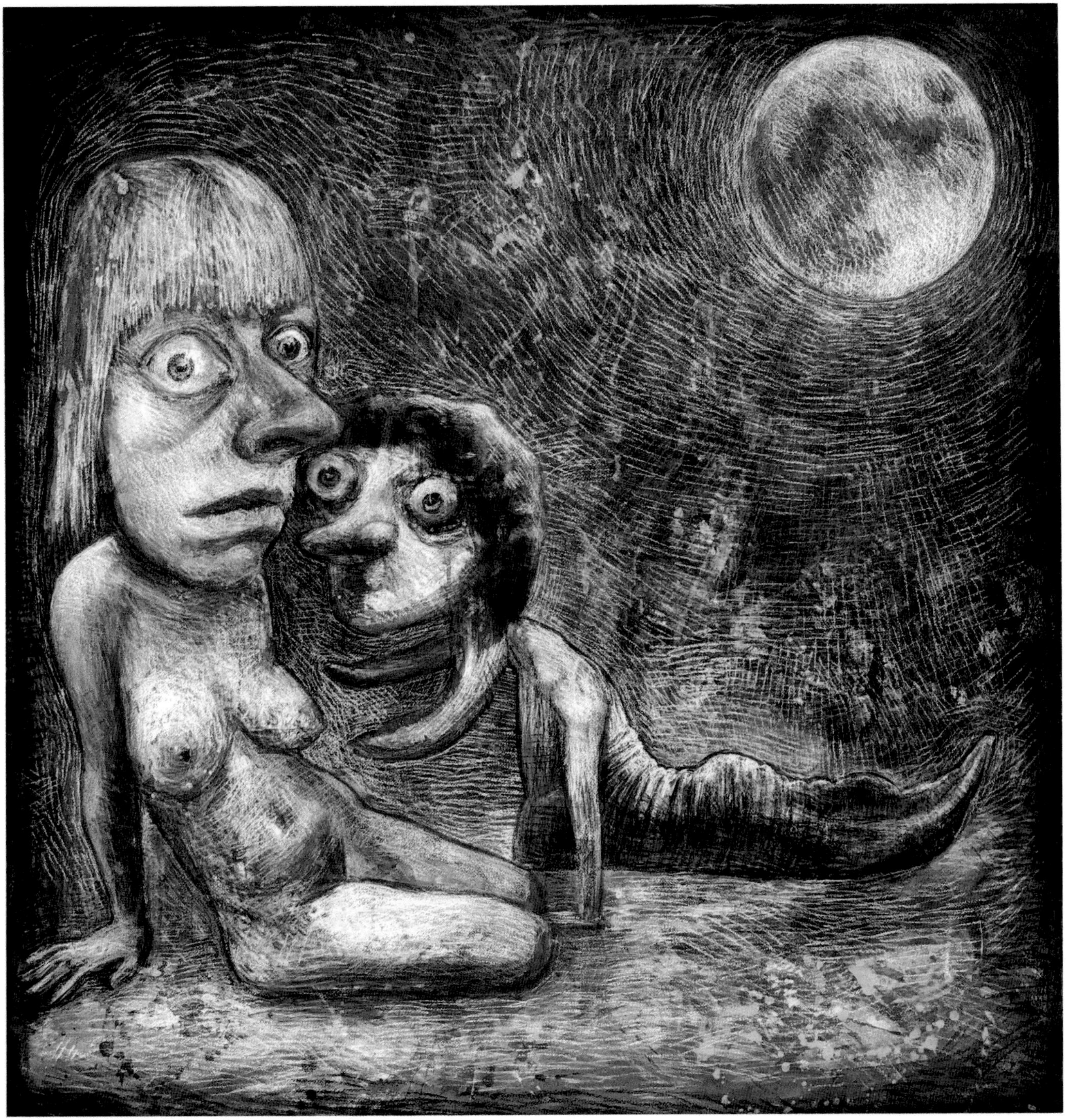

Clown Adrift

Castaway in muddy water—

No joke; dead serious.

Grateful for this little boost

(but I could use a drink).

Out of prayers — I used those up.

Paddling in circles…

I've lost my way.

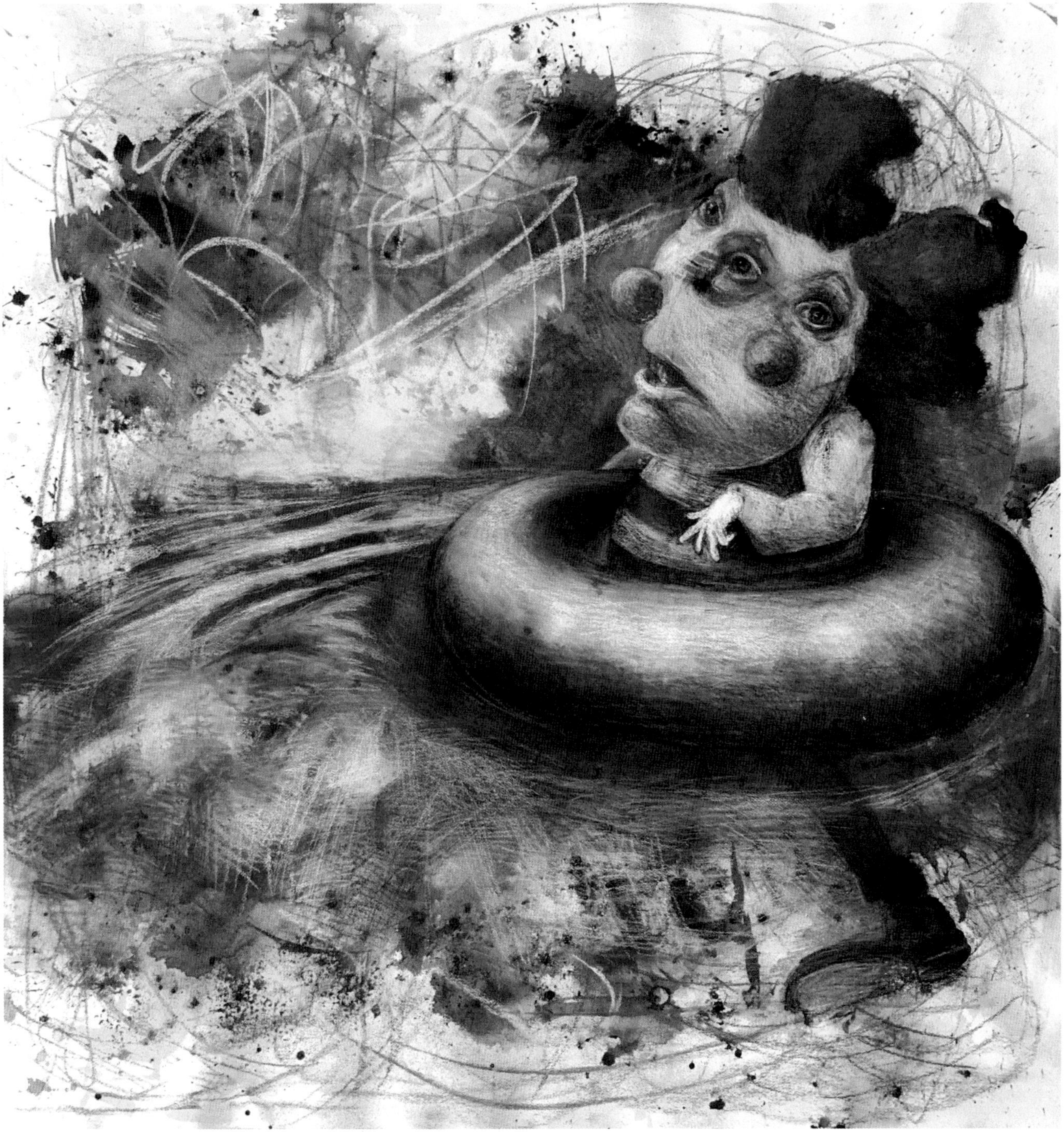

Horsemen of the Apocalypse

Pushing through the crowd,

shouting, marching, stumbling, falling…

No one is in charge.

Disguised as a noble cause,

violence masked as parade.

Boom! One down… no matter…

There's plenty more where they came from.

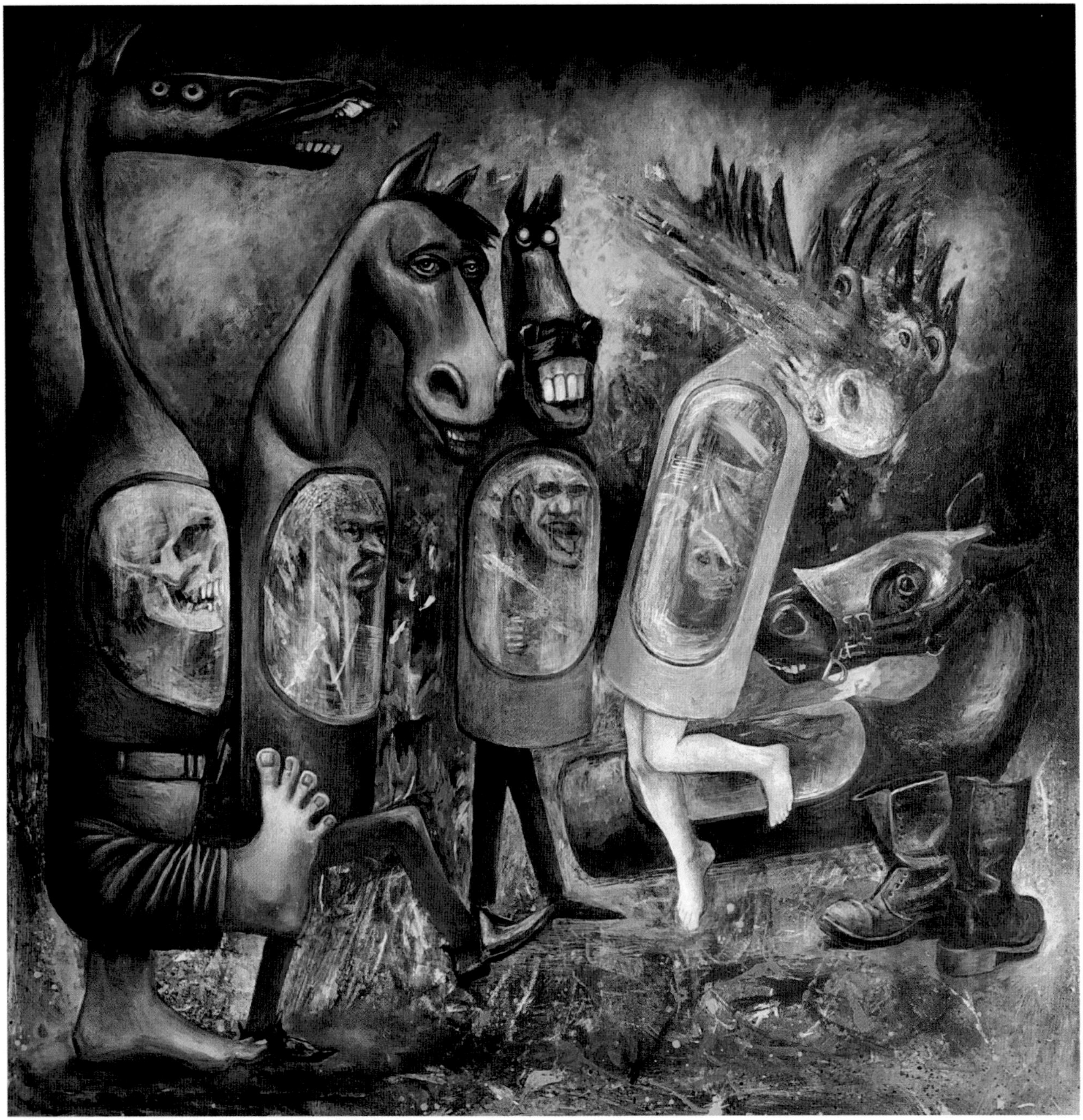

Plucked Grumpy Chicken

Not well read.

Sickly and pale.

Pouting and blue.

Sulking in the corner,

plotting revenge.

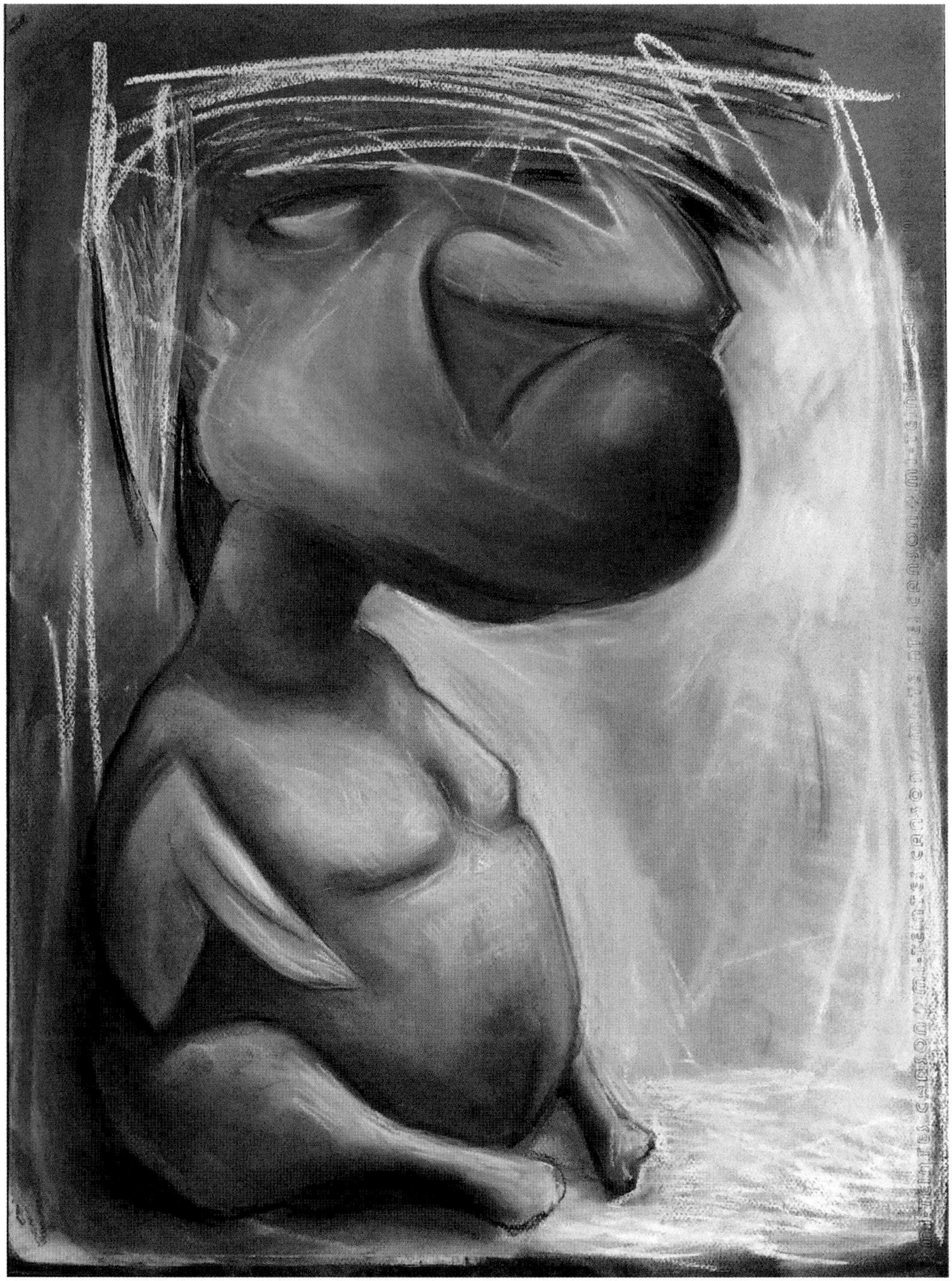

Speeding Back to the Comfort of Hell

Not a minute more:

you can't come with me.

I know a place better than this.

His heart silently told him so.

His mind quietly let him know…

He felt it in his bones.

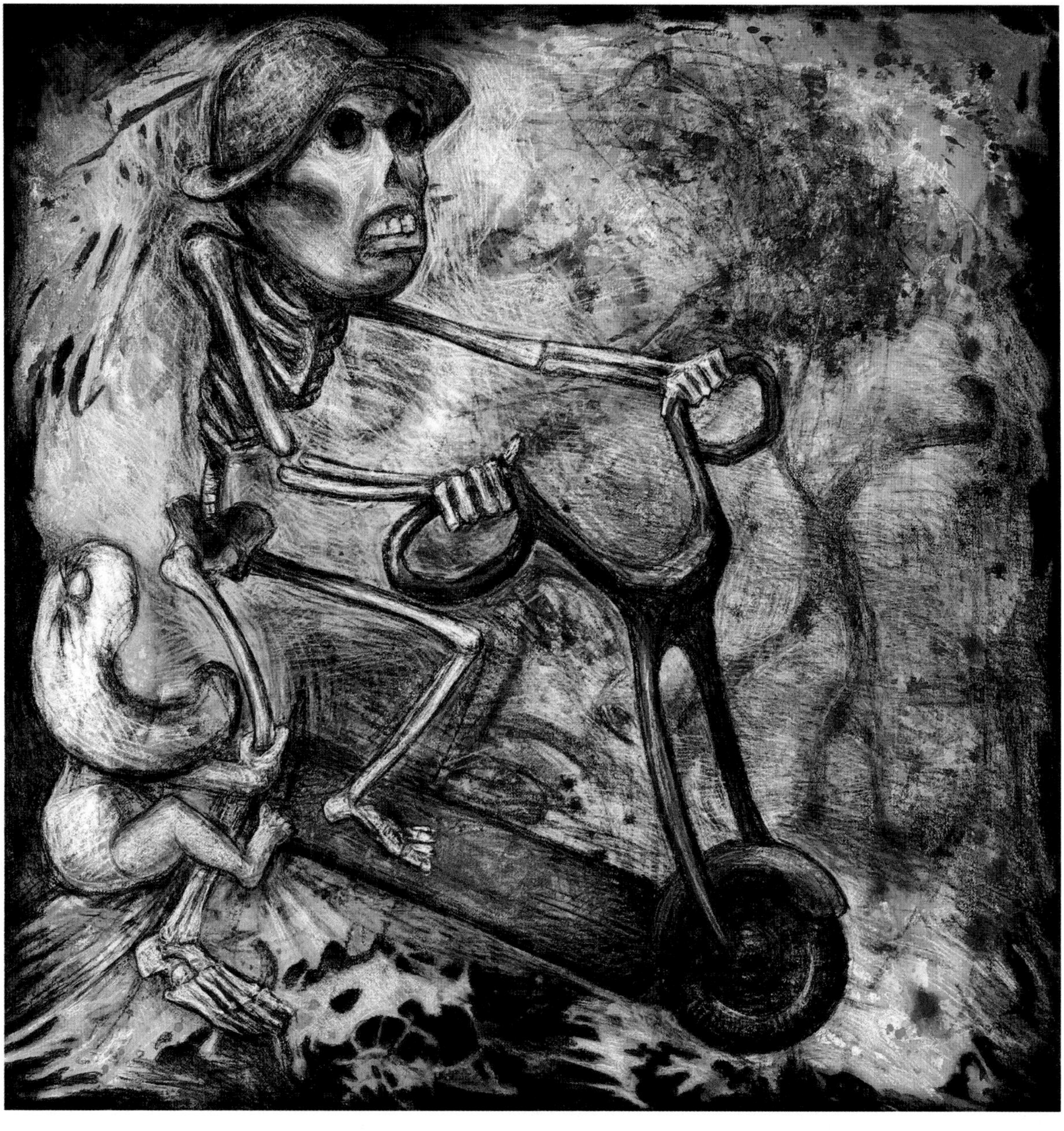

The Crow and the Sparrow
(From Aesop's Fables)

Bit of a chatterbox, am I?

Sorry I mentioned the whole

getting-my-tongue-cut-out and

fleeing-for-my-life thing…

Let's talk about you.

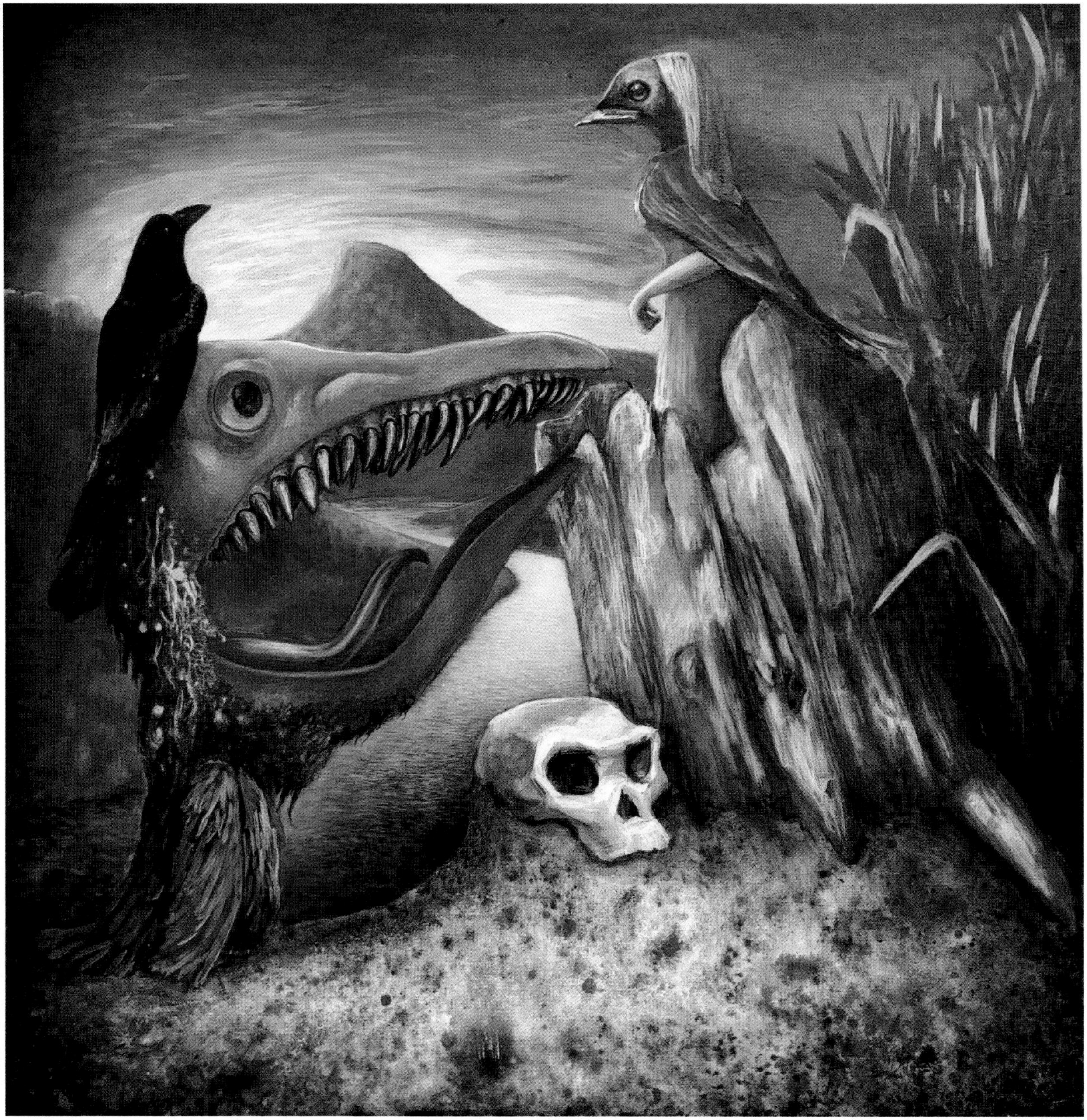

19th Century Belle

Trails of lavender.

The sound of chiffon scratching on a stone-cold floor,

gliding more than walking.

Hiding secrets in crinoline folds,

tightly tied with a yellow satin sash.

Tragic Circus

No one knows why we're here.

The rules keep changing.

The flames… the stench…

The air keeps getting hotter…

If I can only keep my balance

for just a little longer…

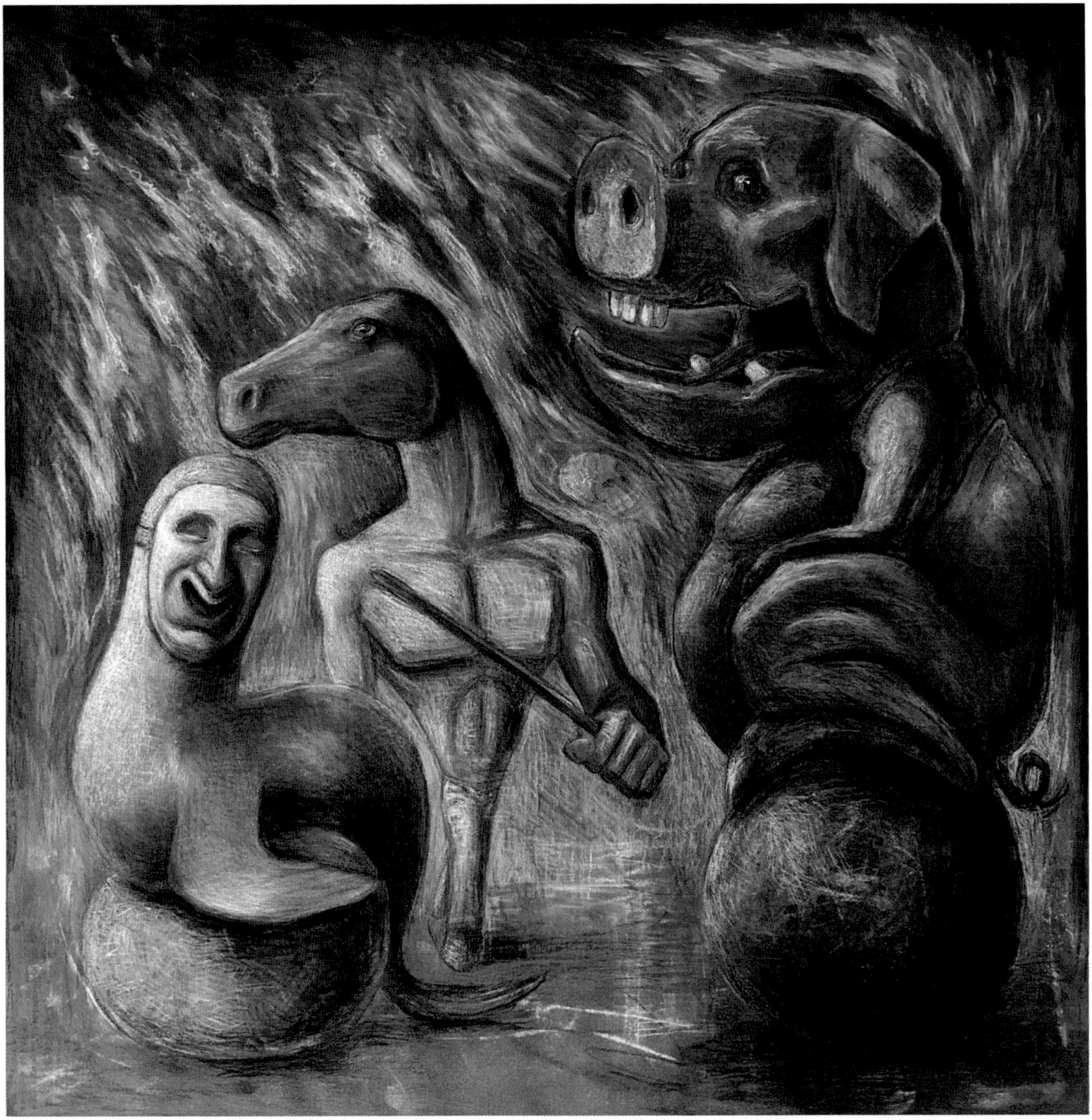

Moon Monster

Pale glowing disc

eclipsed by a fluttering shape—

Whoosh

Was that you?

Was that who?

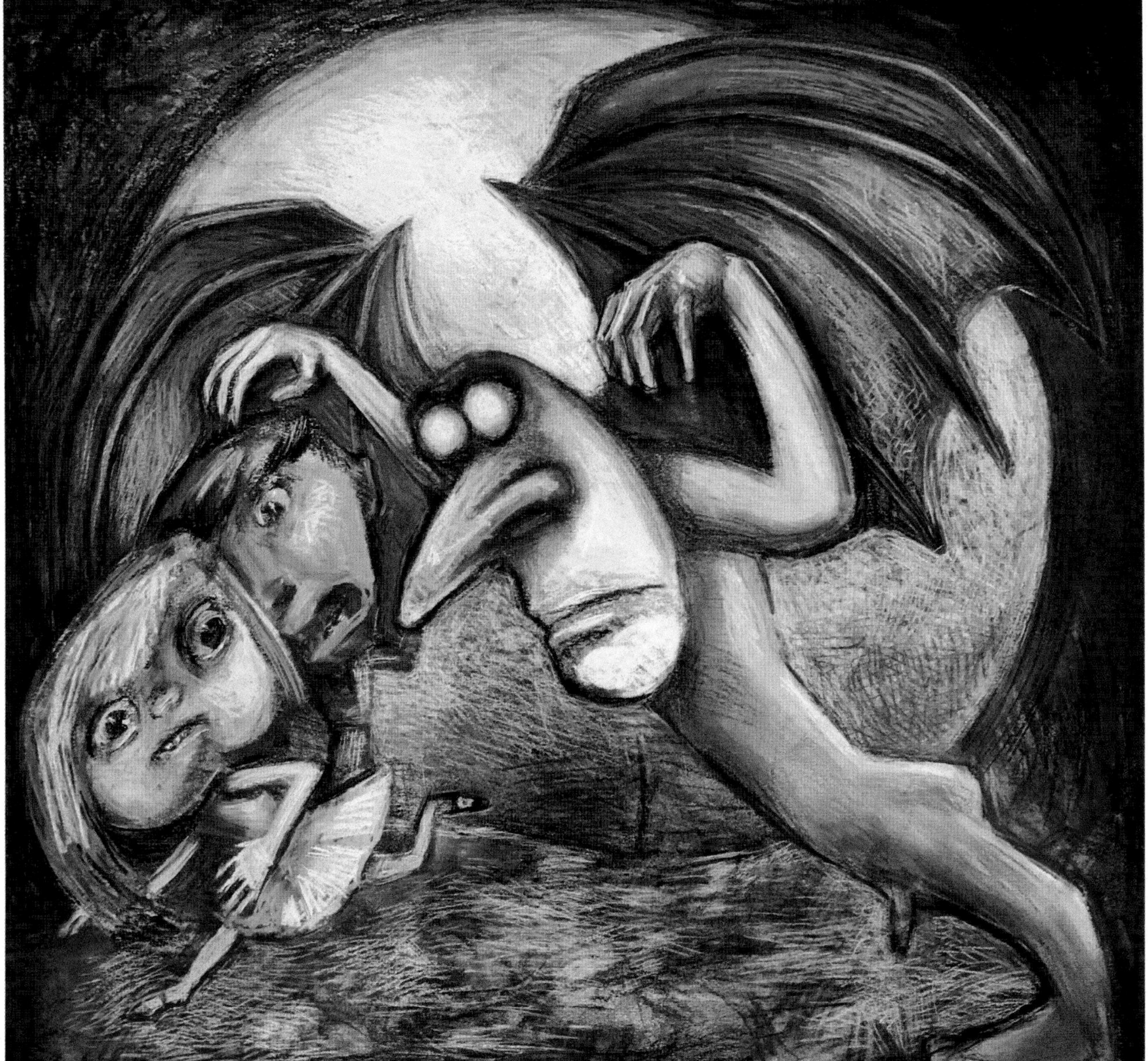

List of Works

03. Lost in a Supermarket - Mixed media on watercolor paper 42” x 42”
05. Domestic Bliss - Mixed media on watercolor paper 45” x 43.5”
07. Thoughts on the Outside - Mixed media on watercolor paper 44” x 45”
07. Destiny Guides Our Fortunes - Mixed media on paper 44” x 44.5”
09. The Young Joker - Acrylic and oil paint on stretched canvas 36” x 36”
11. The Show - Mixed media on watercolor paper 42” x 43”
13. Say No Meore - Acrylic on Canvas 40” x 40”
15. Stand Off on the Island - Mixed media on watercolor paper 37” x 33”
17. The Lamb and the Wolf / Picnic on the Grass - Mixed media on canvas 40” x 40”
19. Fireside Dance - Mixed media on stretched canvas 40” x 40”
21. The Fox and the Mosquitoes - Mixed media on watercolor paper 42” x 42
23. Wolf in Lamb’s Clothing - Pastel on paper 18” x 19”
25. Swamp Thing - Mixed media on watercolor paper 42” x 42”
27. Clown Adrift - Mixed media on watercolor paper 45” x 45”
29. Horsemen of the Apocalypse - Acrylic on canvas 48” x 48”
31. Plucked Grumpy Chicken - Pastel on colored paper 20” x 25”
33. Speeding Back to the Comfort of Hell - Mixed media on watercolor paper 42” x 42”
35. The Crow and the Sparrow - Acrylic on canvas 40” x 40”
37. 19th Century Belle - Mixed media on stretched canvas 30” x 60”
39. Tragic Circus - Mixed media on watercolor paper 42” x 42”
41. Moon Monster - Pastel on paper 21 1/4” x 22 1/2”

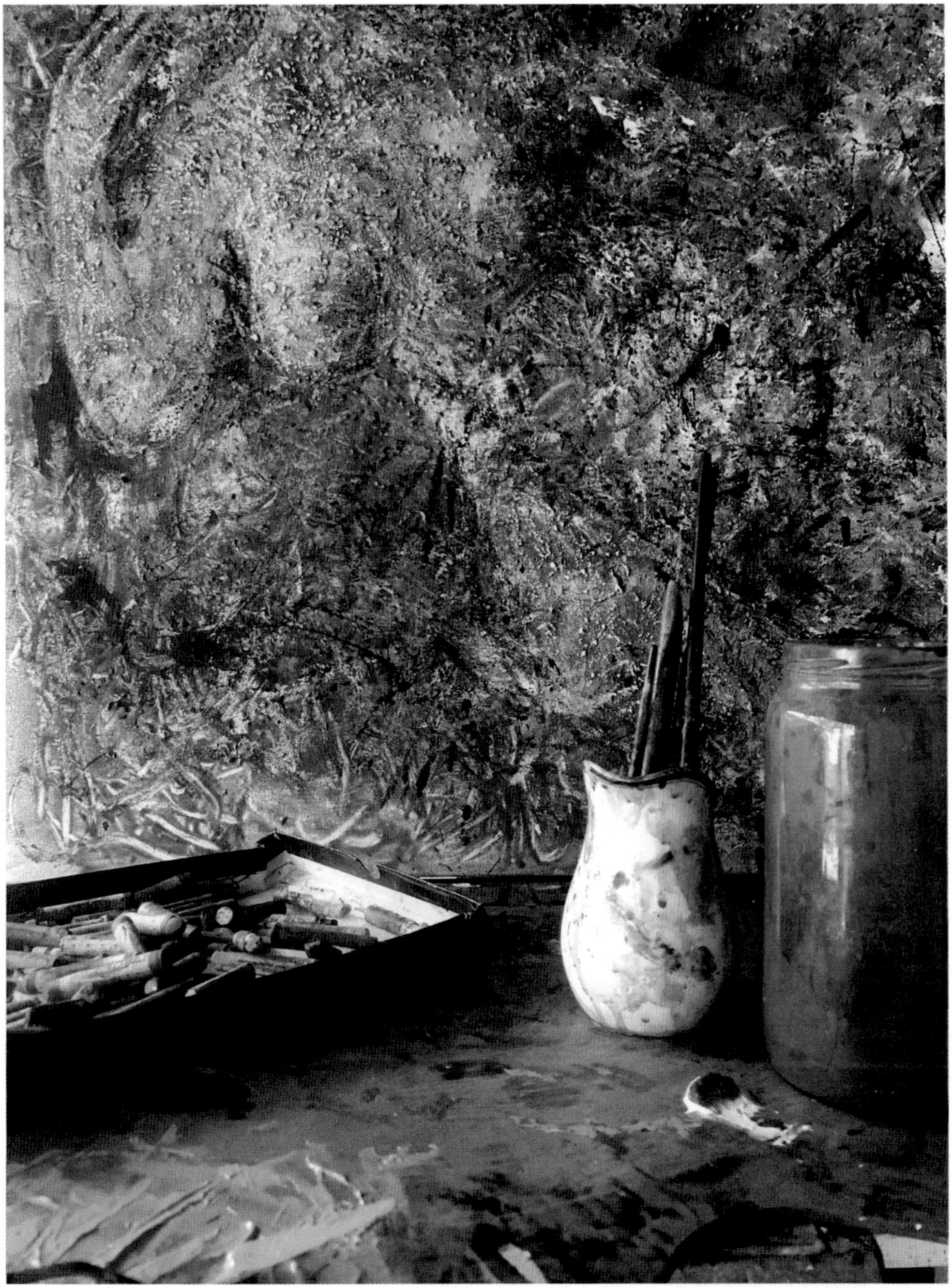

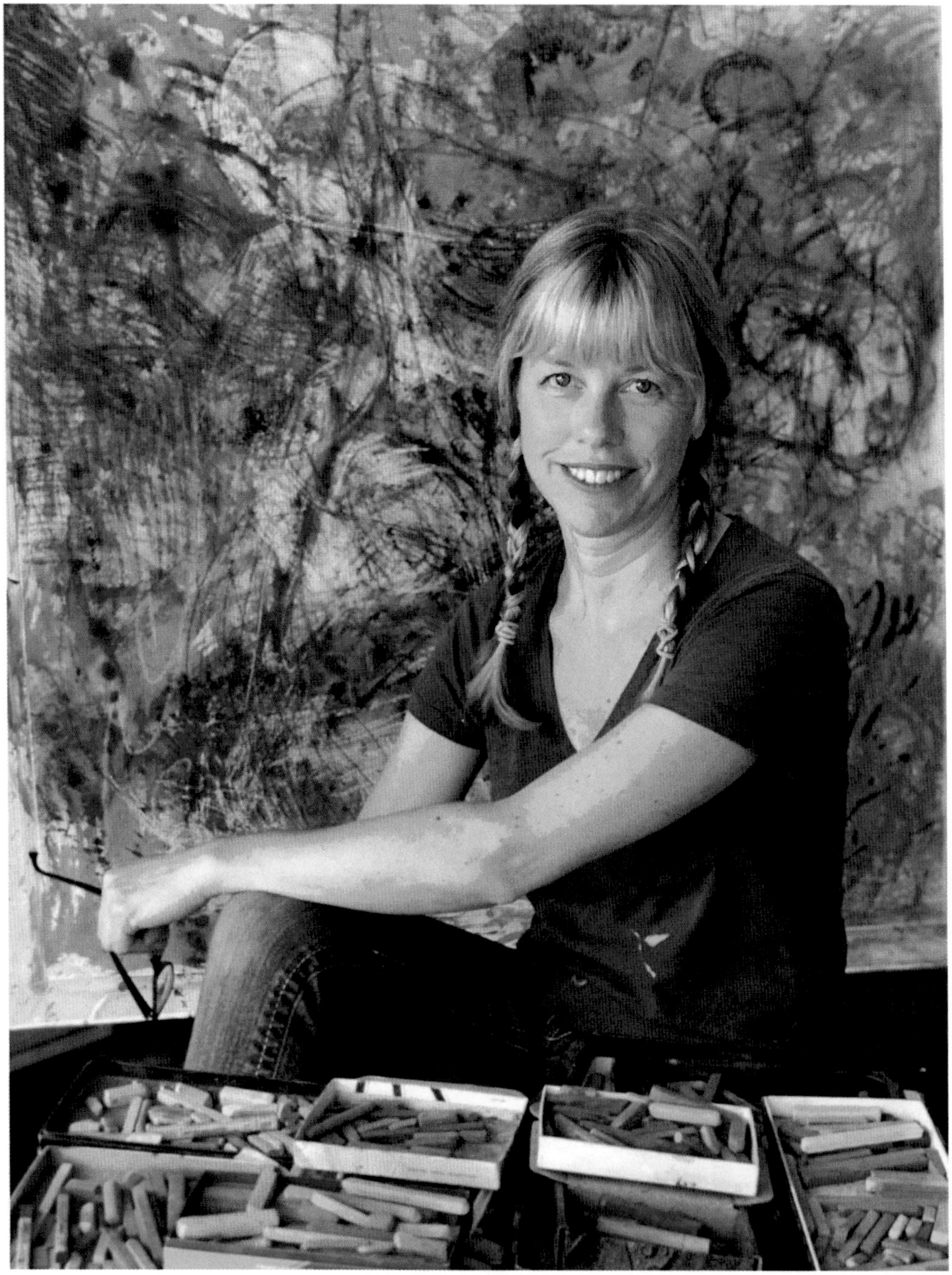

Biography
Nathalie Tierce

Pulling Weeds from a Cactus Garden, is Nathalie Tierce's second book. It follows *Fairy Tale Remnants.* Both were inspired by her mixed media paintings and drawings.

In her career as a professional artist, Ms. Tierce has worked on projects as diverse as productions for Shel Silverstein, Andrew Lloyd Weber, the Rolling Stones, period dramas for the BBC, feature films such as Martin Scorsese's *Shutter Island* and Tim Burton's *Alice in Wonderland,* and painting murals for Disney.

Her relationship to theater and film nurtured her desire to connect with people through storytelling in her visual allegories.

Born and raised in New York City, Nathalie received her formal training at Pratt Institute in New York and The Ecole Nationale Supérieure des Beaux-Arts in Paris. She then spent ten years in Europe refining her craft as a painter.

She maintains a studio in Glendale, CA where she lives with her sculptor husband, son, and two cats.

Indigo Raven

www.nathalietierce.com

Published by Indigo Raven Publishing 350 N Glendale Avenue Ste #306 Glendale CA 91206 ISBN: 9781737832607
©2021 Indigo Publishing ©2021 Nathalie Tierce
Artwork : Nathalie Tierce / Author: Nathalie Tierce / Cover: Nathalie Tierce
Production design: Studio 85 Design - studioeightyfivedesign.com /Art Director: John Buttino